Samuel Stillman Greene

Thought and Expression

The Child's First Book in Written Language

Samuel Stillman Greene

Thought and Expression
The Child's First Book in Written Language

ISBN/EAN: 9783337098339

Printed in Europe, USA, Canada, Australia, Japan

Cover: Foto ©Thomas Meinert / pixelio.de

More available books at **www.hansebooks.com**

THOUGHT AND EXPRESSION

OR

THE CHILD'S FIRST BOOK

IN

WRITTEN LANGUAGE

BY
SAMUEL S. GREENE, LL.D.
AUTHOR OF GREENE'S ANALYSIS AND ENGLISH GRAMMAR

PHILADELPHIA
COWPERTHWAIT & CO.
1877

WESTCOTT & THOMSON,
Stereotypers and Electrotypers. Philada

E. STANLEY HART,
Printer, Philada.

PREFACE.

MOST of our children leave school with little or no practical training in the art of expressing their thoughts with the pen. And such are our methods that most of the remainder will be kept back by a life-long dread of putting their thoughts on paper. Their power of expression by writing is fettered and we fail to set it free.

True, many learn a school penmanship and a school reading, or in the technical sense " learn to read and write." But, whatever may be said of the reading, the writing is not introduced with any immediate reference to *thought*, but as an art of itself. It is usually begun some time after the child has learned to read and spell; it is then taught as the art of making letters and putting them together, not as the art of expressing thought. ˉ Hence it takes on that peculiar style which the taste of the teacher or the rules of the art may determine. It is totally unlike that which the muscles form when under the influence of thought—that which gives a personal character to the hand-writing.

This procedure is equally at variance with nature in calling forth muscular action in speech. The muscles *begin* to act under the impulse of thought, and under the same influence they are exercised and trained. Every child thus acquires his distinctive habit of speaking. There is nothing in the nature of the two cases to occasion this difference. The child can as well learn to write as to speak under the

3

influence of thought, and acquire his penmanship accordingly.

The truth is, nothing but a radical change in the method of *beginning* and *proceeding* will ever enable the mass of our children to wield the written language with ease and freedom. So far as appears to the child, in learning to speak he begins with *expressions of thought* and knows nothing more elementary. Fortunately he is not aware that he really begins with unmeaning letter-sounds, and actually constructs his expressions of thought by combining these. He does it by an unconscious process to which it is best, for the present, he should not be awakened, lest the needed voluntary effort to connect thought with language should thereby be embarrassed.

It is here that the common method appears in its true light. It seeks to make the child intensely awake to unmeaning elements and disturbing processes at the very beginning. It regards reading as a sound-producing rather than a thought-receiving process, and writing as a word-making rather than a thought-expressing process. Any act of conscious spelling so preoccupies the mind as to leave little room for the meaning of the words employed. But what shall be said when the spelling has for its chief aim, not the meaning but the *utterance* of the words? It becomes a positive diversion from thought, leaving that as something wholly incidental. What nature seeks to conceal (elements) at the beginning our method of spelling seeks to reveal, and what nature seeks to reveal (thought) our method most effectually conceals.

The method here proposed follows the plan of nature. It teaches the child to *write* as well as read, to combine elements into *expressions of thought* in writing as in speaking, and with as little regard to the elements themselves,—to receive thought from combined elements in reading as in hearing, and with a like freedom from any distracting analysis or hinderance from spelling; in short, to make reading and writing what they really are, correlative and auxiliary processes—the one to draw thought from written language, the other to put thought into it. It is adapted to the child as soon as he can make and interpret *forms* or groups of marks as he made and interpreted groups of sounds. He should know as little of letters now as he knew of letter-sounds then, that he may combine the former as unwittingly now as he did the latter then. At first he merely makes groups of letters stand for *thought*, but will ere long find that the letters themselves stand for *sounds*.

In the transition from spoken to written language the method is *initiatory*, furnishing the very first step which the child should take. He may and should have previous object lessons on form. Having completed the First Book, he is prepared for the First Reader of any series, as also for the Second Book in writing, which follows this to unfold a series of true Language Lessons—not for the purpose of introducing the technical terms of grammar, but for teaching the proper forms of writing the language for the practical affairs of life.

The fundamental idea of the whole plan is that the child *begins* with the only essential use of language as the expression of thought, and *proceeds* by forming a *permanent habit* of writing, as he did of speaking.

INTRODUCTION.

EXPLANATION OF THE METHOD.

CHILDREN and the mass of mankind make use of language only as an instrument for the expression of thought. They put thought into it and draw thought from it with scarcely a passing notice of the instrument itself. Such is its normal use. But when they are made to think of the language itself, whether in spelling, reading, reciting or committing to memory, their attention to words defeats the very end for which language is given, and so renders its use abnormal. Such use often becomes habitual, as in learning to read, and shows itself in a meaningless utterance of mere words. The aim of the method here proposed is to teach the written language from the start as *the expression of thought*.

Language in its normal use does not come to the child as letter-sounds, syllables and words to be put together, but as these already put together. At first it greets his ears as the Chinese does ours—a mere jumble of unmeaning sounds —just as now the written page greets his eye as an array of unmeaning marks.

It was no analytic scheme of the philosopher, but the native instinct of the mother, that first taught him to draw thought from these combined sounds. Calling attention to herself or to some object near, she would say, " Here is mamma," " Here is kitty," " Here is Jennie." This object, with her own gestures and winning smiles, was gradually giving significance, not to these letter-sounds, not to these syllables, not to these words as such, but to these *idioms* or *groups of sounds*. It was these *combined sounds* that gradually associated themselves with his thought-pictures, the charming objects of the world within him. At length, without object or gesture, these sounds themselves or their significant parts—never anything more elementary—became expressions of thought *to* him whenever heard.

This, however, was but one part of a double process; soon arose an irresistible desire to produce these sounds whenever the objects were at hand or the pictures presented themselves to his mind's eye. To his ear and to his mind these sounds were familiar, not as separated, but as put together; yet his undeveloped organs of speech were too feeble to put them all together at once. At first he did well if he stammered "papa" when he meant, "There is papa." Ere long he could say, "Da papa," and after weeks of practice, "There is papa." Though he learned gradually to put words together by a seeming syntactic process, he was really gaining the use of a newly-developed faculty on words already put together. At length oral language became expression of thought *to* him when *heard*, and *from* him when *spoken*.

How can *written* language best become expression of thought *to* him and *from* him? Not by learning to *read* it merely, not by learning to *write* it merely, not by learning to read or write it as the expression of *sound* alone or chiefly, but by learning both to read and write it as the expression of *thought* chiefly and of *sound* incidentally. In other words, though the written language is the expression of sound as well as of thought, it should be *learned* as the direct expression of thought; it should be to the eye and hand what the spoken language is to the ear and tongue.

No intervening process, as that of conscious spelling, either alphabetic or phonic, should be allowed to hinder the direct association of thought with the written expression. Ordinary spelling is a logical process requiring analysis and synthesis. Yet difficult as it is, it would receive some justification if it furnished any aid in associating written language with *thought.* On the contrary, its immediate aim is to associate written language with *sound,* and so it becomes a positive interruption to thought. The child who has just endured the strain of his undeveloped logical faculty in bringing together the sounds of a word is in no mood for calling up a well-formed thought-picture. He has done enough to *pronounce* the word. But is he to learn the words without spelling? By no means; he is to learn them by a tacit, unobtrusive, unconscious spelling, just as he learned the spoken words.

How is this to be? Nature suggests the way. In her method there is no recognition of sounds or groups of sounds below those which have significance. No mother ever dreams of helping her child to speak *dog,* for example, by analyzing it or by resorting to a process of phonic spelling, even though the philosopher insist that the child must make three muscular efforts, and thereby produce and combine three elementary sounds in order to speak it. What is that to her or to her child in his struggles to express his thought? Nature represses all thought of elementary sounds; in fact, it is by this very repression that combined sounds can become expression of thought. All elements and all combining processes are wisely hidden lest by rising into full consciousness they divert attention from thought. The child learns unwittingly to speak (spell) the elements into the words and think the meaning of these without stopping to think of the elements themselves or of what he does with them.

Let him then take *graphic* instead of *phonic* elements—that is, letters instead of letter-sounds. Let him *write* (spell) these, unwittingly (as letters) into the words—simply *make* and *see* the words as something significant, without stopping to think of letters or how he uses them; let him give attention to the meaning of the words—at present to nothing more elementary—and he is in the true way of learning the written as he learned the spoken language. He simply learns to put forth his own thoughts by means of combined marks as he did by combined sounds when learning to speak, and thus begins with the best spelling he will ever learn—just such as he will need in all the affairs of life, just such as the best writers and printers employ, *all* the spelling, in fact, that he will need for the present in learning to read and write.

In thus putting marks together as he once put sounds together without explicitly knowing what he is doing, he only obeys a fundamental law of nature, as also of the great Teacher—namely, the law of *doing* in order to *know*, not, as in the common method, that of knowing in order to do. He follows the true philosophy and yet is aware of no philosophy ; he acquires an unconscious synthesis to render possible a future analysis. Writing, like speaking, *necessitates* a *combination*, not a full recognition, of elements. He *makes* the language for the purposes of thought, and afterward by a gradual analysis comes to know it as it is in itself. Thus, his pre-scientific attainments become so inwrought that his future scientific knowledge may be evolved from an experience of his own, and not slavishly adopted from that of another. He exalts thought and subordinates the mere processes of language. Analysis, rigid and thorough, is yet in store for him.

He thus learns to write by writing, to read by reading, just as he learned to speak by speaking, to hear by hearing, just as he must learn to swim by swimming. He must plunge in and trust to the instincts of his nature and the example of others *to find out how*, not wait *to know how* before he even *begins* to learn how.

But what he repeatedly *makes* as the expression of thought he instantly *recognizes* as the expression of thought. This advantage from *doing* (actually *making* the expression) is denied to those who do not learn to *write* as they learn to read. Reading is not the art of spelling and *pronouncing,* as many suppose, but the art of receiving thought at sight of its written expression. In fact, when thought is once awakened by visible signs, just as in our own spontaneous thinking, it may or may not be uttered. If uttered, we call it *reading aloud* in one case and *talking* in the other. The first step in all true reading is the *silent* reception of thought from a *glance* at the written language. The utterance is *incidental* and should be prompted by the presence and inward impulse of thought. Utterance from mere spelling should never be called reading.

Thus the question is answered. Written language may become expression *from* and *to* the child only by learning *to write* as well as read, and to do both for thought primarily and chiefly for sound really, yet incidentally; it then becomes to the eye and hand what the spoken language is to the ear and tongue.

As soon as the child enters upon this course he is on the way to a more scientific knowledge of the language as such. He cannot long write the oft-repeated letters without asking what they are and what they are called; he cannot long put them into words in an invariable order without feeling that any other order is wrong; he cannot make and pronounce such words as *cat, rat, bat, mat, sat, hat* without perceiving that written words, through their letters, represent spoken words. In the mean time, he has lost in nothing but has gained in everything—in reading, in writing, in the true art of spelling and in the use of language as the instrument of thought. He has given due prominence to the thought-element at the very start, and comes to a knowledge of the sound-element gradually but surely. How much better for his future than if this order were reversed !

In all this he is never without *guidance.* But at first,

both in the words and in the idioms, his guidance is wholly *external.* He copies the models with unquestioning fidelity, and thereby gradually discovers resemblances, differences, uniform changes and countless analogies which become inwardly suggestive. At length these give rise to a permanent *impression,* a sort of *linguistic instinct,* which, though never infallible, is of the highest value in the use of language, written as well as oral. It is prompt to utter its unobtrusive protest, " That does not look right," whenever the spelling or construction is wrong.

Thus out of his own experience he may gradually evolve a scientific grammar of the language. But if he never does this, he may become a good writer, may keep his accounts, transact his business, carry on his correspondence, prepare reports, write advertisements and paragraphs for the press—may do anything required in good writing—only he may not be a critic and may not always *know* when he is right or wrong, He will, however, escape that untold loss which the present method entails upon all who must cut short their school education.

One thing more should be said. Language, as the word indicates, is *tongue*-work, and not *hand*-work. The children need drill-practice on *form* before they touch the pen or pencil. No better plan than that of the Kindergarten can be devised—namely, that of placing sticks of measured lengths so as to train the eye and hand in creating the various forms. For the same purpose these forms should be drawn upon the slate. Lessons of this kind ought to precede any attempt at reading or writing. Not only this, but *conversation,* free, assuring and inspiring, should be resorted to at all times as the chief means of awakening and drawing forth thought.

Suggestions to the Teacher.

NEVER ask a hesitating child to *spell* a word for its pronunciation, but to *write* it for its meaning, and thus secure *both;* for he who writes a word must spell it, and he who knows the meaning of any familiar word can pronounce it.

2. Make the thought the chief thing and the act of expression a kind of incidental necessity, and thus lead the child imperceptibly through what might otherwise be an irksome task. Keep up the child's *delight* in expressing thought by making it as fresh when written as when spoken. Let all the drill exercises and all the criticisms which are intended to secure correctness of expression be carried on in the interest of thought. The language should be good not so much for its own sake as for the thought which it embodies.

3. Keep constantly in mind the three stages through which the child must pass—the *copying stage*, or that in which he *imitates* the model again and again under the special guidance of the teacher and is drilled with unabating fidelity; the *memory stage*, or that in which the sufficiency or insufficiency of the copying is tested by an appeal to the mental model; the *mastery stage*, or that in which all effort of memory ceases and the written expression, like the spoken, comes to mind spontaneously.

12

4. Let the children use the script letters in writing and reading. In the earlier reading lessons the script and Roman letters are used together that the children may catch the latter by their similarity to the former. It may be thought best to use at first the Roman or to make the script so conform to it as to render the resemblance more striking. The teacher's own experience will be the best guide. By all means eventually teach them to make what they will hereafter *use* in reading and writing, and to *grasp from resemblance*, so far as may be, what they will use for the most part only in reading.

5. Use the blackboard incessantly; make it copybook, speller, dictionary and grammar, and yet without seeming to be either. Let the lessons be increased by adding new words whenever the children can bear it, and by all means *divide the given lessons* if they are found too long. Fortunately, the teacher has at hand a *sure test:* they can write from memory what they have copied sufficiently. Frequent reviews will be found indispensable, and these will give *constant employment* even to the youngest classes.

6. As soon as possible make the new method of expressing thought *practical* and *useful* by permitting and encouraging the children to present their requests to the teacher in writing, or to make a record of anything that interests them.

7. At all times seize upon the peculiar advantages of the *method.* It is neither the *word-method* nor the *spelling-method*, and yet it combines the excellences and avoids the faults of both. The child learns no word without spelling it, and spells no word for the sake of learning it. He spells it for thought and learns it from spelling, yet the spelling and the learning are so incidental and unobtrusive that it becomes at once the sign of thought.

8. Not only so, but enter into *the spirit of the method.*

Become to the children in the written language what the mother was to her child in the spoken. Know nothing but *language as expression of thought.* Then no emergency can arise which will not be readily met. What mother, whether from the city or the desert, ever fails to give her own language to her child? Progress will be measured, not by the number of verbal forms acquired, but by the facility with which living thought is put into written form.

9. Let criticism cease to be the work of a detective, seizing upon every violation of law; let it rather be that of a friend seeking to make the child a law unto himself. Let the standards be, not the abstract canons of the books, but the practical examples of *good usage.* Let these be presented in actual instances for the inspection of the children, and let the attention be called to those points which are especially to be impressed. Let the appeal be made to that instinctive insight for which children are especially noted. Thus they will see what competent authority *does,* rather than commit to memory what a book *says.* Usage will be their guide in the written as in the spoken language. "Every one writes so" will be as authoritative as " Every one speaks so," and the teacher has only day by day to represent this authority.

PART I.

EXPRESSIONS FOR OBJECTS.

LESSON 1.

See the dog.

See   the   dog.

____ ____ *dog.*

Method.—*1.* Make the thought *vivid* and *real* by object, picture or description. Point out and read the two full lines, each child tracing the line. Read the third, "See the," in a low tone, but "**dog**" with emphasis.

2. Write in script on the board "**dog.**" Do it slowly, plainly, with open letter resembling the Roman or ordinary printed letter, at first. Then point to the picture, and to the printed and written word, saying **dog.**

3. The children, separately and together, *speak* "**dog.**" Teacher says, You *speak* "**dog**" to tell what you think, but I *write* "dog" (writing at the same time) to tell what I think. In the next lesson *you* may write it. How many would like to do it?

Note.—The lesson proper for the child is in large type. He is supposed to know nothing of the "Method" or notes in small type, except

15

LESSON 2.

___ ___ *dog.*

Method.—1. Teacher at the board goes over Lesson I. as before, and says, See how I write "dog," making the parts distinctly, but saying nothing of letters, spelling or anything else but this new way of expressing thought.

2. Children with slate and pencil imitate the model awkwardly, roughly and almost illegibly, it may be, but quite as well as they first spoke it.

Suggestions.—The teacher will realize the advantage of encouraging words at this moment of triumph, as when the mother caught the first word from the child's lips. Cheer them on, make much of this new way of telling their thoughts, nothing at all of parts or processes Urge them on directly to the main object—namely, that of *giving* and *receiving thought* from written language. The fundamental rule is—as when they were learning to speak—*Repeat*, REPEAT, REPEAT, till the forms are permanently impressed. Let them copy this word many times and preserve their work for examination. This gives them *something to do* at once.

___

as they come to him through the teacher. The teacher will do well to *study* and *follow* the Method until her experience suggests a better, remembering that the *language* in small type is for *her*, not the child, and that *hers* is for the guidance of the *child*. He is accustomed to take *oral* language, not *as* language, but as thought in language. That he may not take written language as mere language, every possible exertion should be made to give freshness and prominence to the thought. Hence no formulated rules should at present be committed to memory as *language*. When the child has repeated a process many times, he may *tell* what he has done; *that* is true expression.

LESSON 3.

(Reading.)	*(Writing.)*
——— ——— *dog.*	—— *the dog.*
——— ——— dog.	

Method.—1. Let the children read the first expression first from their slates as something which they have made to stand for *dog ;* then from the first line in the book as the same; then from the second, as something like theirs. Let them catch the word at a glance, the eye following the order in which they made the word. Allow no hesitation, as if they were spelling. Let them speak it, as when they really see a dog or are thinking of one. Thus, let them *begin right in reading.*

2. Let them write the example, *the dog*, the teacher saying nothing of putting two words together, of the space between them, or of the period at the end; but be sure that they copy everything. They will thus *begin correctly in writing.* Let them copy this many times, as above.

2

LESSON 4.

(Reading.) | **(Writing.)**

——— ——— *dog.* | *See the dog.*

——— ——— dog. | *See* ——— ———.

——— *the dog.* |

——— the dog. | ——— *the dog.*

Method.—1. Read the first and second example, as in Lesson III.; read the third and fourth as one expression, " the dog," not " the—dog." Bring into a single group the words which express a single thought. Never allow the words to be isolated, as when children consciously spell them.

2. Teacher writes on the board " See;" children *imitate* without a word about capitals. Teacher writes after " See," with a suitable space, " the ;" children imitate. The teacher carefully inspects their work to make the imitation as exact as possible. In like manner insert " dog."

3. Give drill-practice, while keeping in mind this whole idiom for *calling attention to objects.* Write first " See ——— ———;" then "the dog," and so on. Encourage them to imitate accurately, but promptly. Impress the whole expression firmly and make them familiar with it.

Note.—Hitherto the blanks have indicated a suppression of parts which the mind and voice could readily furnish. They suggest that the whole idiom has a *form* which must be kept in mind. They will have the same value hereafter, but with the further meaning that they are to be actually filled by writing. Let the children copy what is written and supply the rest.

LESSON 5.

(Reading.) | **(Writing.)**

(Reading.)	(Writing.)
___ ___ *dog.*	*See the* ___.
___ ___ dog.	*See the cat.*
___ *the dog.*	___ *the cat.*
___ the dog.	*See the* ___.
See the dog.	*See the pig.*
See the dog.	___ *the pig.*
	See ___ *pig.*

Method.—1. Let the pupils read the first two lines *silently* for the thought, then let them *speak* naturally, as they would their own thoughts. Proceed in the same way with the second and third two lines. Let the *reading* be thought-receiving, and the *speaking* thought-uttering.

2. Teacher writes on the board "See the," and then says, *What?* Pupils may now *speak* and tell what object can be put in place of *dog.* From the pictures they will be likely to say *cat, pig,* but they may be made to add many others from such *thought-pictures* as will come to mind. The more vivid these are, the better; they will create a sense of *want.* How shall we *write* " ox," " horse," " boy," etc.?

LESSON 6.
(Reading.)

____ *the dog.*	*See the dog.*
____ the dog.	See the dog.
____ *the cat.*	*See the cat.*
____ the cat..	See the cat.
____ *the pig.*	*See the pig.*
____ the pig.	See the pig.

***Note.*—**At all times before dismissing the class assign a suitable review lesson for them to write at their seats. Let their work be read and examined. It is the period for *forming habits;* let them be so good as never to need correcting. This idiom opens a wide field for the blank " See the ——." Occasionally new words such as help make up the *idiomatic forms* will appear for the first time in the *reading lesson.*

(Writing.)

O, see the cat!

O, see the ___ !

O, see ___ ___ !

___ see ___ ___ !

Look at the ___ (what?)

O, ___ ___ the frog!

___ ___ ___ pig!

Method.—*1.* Let the children read from their books, from their slates, and from examples written spontaneously by the teacher on the board.

2. Teacher may say something like this: When we see anything that excites our feelings suddenly, we often *speak out*, O, and talk earnestly; but when we *write*, we make these marks (teacher writes *O*, and places this mark (!) at the end) to show that we are in earnest. Now look at this picture; you would say, "O, see the cat!" You may now write it as I do.

Suggestion.—In all these examples it is everything to the child *to see* just how the *teacher* makes the expressions. Work *with* the children and *for* them. Make them feel that they are really *telling* something. Take pains to connect the words with *thought*, and they will soon be connected with *sound*. If any wish to know the name of a letter (as O, here) give it.

LESSON 7.
(Reading.)

See the frog and the cat!

See the frog and the cat!

O, see the dog and the pig!

O, see the dog and the pig!

O, look! the pig! the cat!

O, look! the pig! the cat!

(Writing.)

Here is
the ____.

Here is the rat.

Here is ____ ____.

Is the cat here?

Is ____ ____ here?

O, here is the rat!

O, ____ ____ ____ ____!

Here is ____ ____ and ____ ____.

Suggestion.—The teacher will draw attention to the tones of voice when we *speak* to ask anything, and will then show how we *write* to ask, as in the fifth line: Great care should be taken that every *distinctive mark* (here (?)) be faithfully imitated. The change of idiom to that of *the object near* need not be named to the children. They perceive it intuitively.

LESSON 8.

(Reading.)

O, see the rat!

O, see the rat!

O, look! here is the dog.

O, look! here is the dog.

O, see the cat and the dog!

O, see the cat and the dog!

Here is the cat.

Here is the cat.

Is the frog here?

Is the frog here?

No, here is the dog.

No, here is the dog.

O, here is a cat, or a dog!

O, here is a cat, or a dog!

Suggestion.—See Note, Lesson VI. Be sure that the children read *a cat*, not a—cat. (See Method, Less. IV.) The blank to be filled by oral practice still pertains to the *object* (what?). The *idiomatic formula* " Here is ——," will soon be mastered.

(Writing.)

Do you see that ___?

___ ___ see that mouse?

Yes; I do see that mouse.

Yes; ___ do see ___ ___.

Is not this a ___?

Do you see this boy?

Is this ___ ___?

O, see ___ ___!

Can I see this ___?

Yes; you can see this girl and that boy.

Suggestion.—The teacher will call upon the children to *speak*, then *write*, any other words for the blanks : as, " Do you see the *cat, dog, mouse, pig*," etc.   If it should be found that new words come in too fast for the children, take only one or two of them.

LESSON 9.
(Reading.)

[Let the children read from their slates and in review of Lessons VI. and VII.]

(Writing.)

There is that ___.

Is that fox there?

Yes; that fox is there.

O, there is that fox!

O, ___ ___ that ___ !

Do look at him.

Where is the dog?

Where is ___ ___ ?

The dog is not there.

Is the fox there?

Is ___ ___ there?

Yes; the ___ is there.

Dictation.—How many of you can *think* just how to write *dog?* You may all close your books and write *dog, cat, pig.* How many can write, "*See the dog*"? Let all try it.

Suggestion.—Impress the idiomatic form, " There is ——," and let them fill the blank orally. The children are now prepared, at least, to begin upon the second stage of their work. It will give rise to special sharpness of attention when they feel that they must *remember* what they copy from sight. Hereafter the attempt to recall should be made at every Lesson.

The teacher may gradually, and without formality, *impress* upon the mind the *characteristics* of the idioms ; thus, "Suppose the object were *near*, what would you *say* or *write?*" "Suppose it were *at a distance* or *out of sight?*" They will soon recognize "*Here is* ——," "*There is* ——," "*Where is* ——?*"

LESSON 10.

(Reading.)

Do you see that mouse?

Do you see that mouse?

O, yes; I see that mouse.

O, yes; I see that mouse.

Where is the cat?

Where is the cat?

Here is the cat.

Here is the cat.

Can the cat see the mouse?

Can   the   cat   see   the   mouse ?

Where is the rat?

Where   is   the   rat ?

Is the dog there?

Is   the   dog   there ?

Can the dog see the rat?

Can   the   dog   see   the   rat ?

(Writing.)

Ann, may I see that rose?

___, may I

___ ___ ___?

Yes, Ned; you may see this rose.

Yes, —— ; you may —— ——.

O, look! look! a rat!

O, where is the rat?

Will the rat bite?

Will —— —— ——?

Shall we run?

Shall __ __?

Yes; we must run.

Yes; we __ __.

Dictation.—Cat; the dog; this rat; a pig; see the rat. [Give any other expressions which the children are able to write from memory. It is important to press forward this part of their work. They gain rapidly after they can write from memory.]

--- ◦◦ ---

LESSON 11.

(*Reading.*)

See the dog and the pig. Where is the dog? The dog is here. Where is the pig? There is the pig. Can the pig run? Yes; the pig will run. Can the pig see the dog? Yes; the pig can see the dog, and the dog can see the pig. O, see! see! poor pig!

[Let the children read also from their slates and from the board.]

(Writing.)

Do you see that boy and
that girl? No; I do
not see the boy or the girl.

No; I __ not __ __ __
or __ __ .

Where is the boy, and
where is the girl?
O, now I
see the boy
and the girl!

O, look at those boys!

O, look at ___ ___ !

How many boys are there?

How many ___ ___ ___ ?

There are two boys.

There ___ ___ ___ .

O, see! see! the hen and the chickens!

3

How many chickens are there?

There are one, two, three, four, five, six chickens!

Will a chicken catch a fly?

Dictation.—Here is the pig.   See the rose.   O, there is the hen!
[Give some six or eight examples.   Keep up an *incessant* drill-practice
that the thought may be permanently *impressed* (pressed in) as if into
the idiomatic form, just as the seal-image is pressed into the wax.   It is
only in this way that thought can be *expressed* (pressed out)—that is,
from the mind into the idiom—and thus made to manifest itself out-
wardly as the seal-image does in the wax.   Let the impression be *strong*
and *permanent*.   The teacher will see that the chief object is to make
an indelible impression of the *thought-picture* upon the written words
before much is said of *sounds*.   Printed pictures are mere substitutes or
auxiliaries.   The minds of the children can readily be trained to associate with words far better pictures than the artist can make.   Any
good plan which will interest the children in *thought* is always desirable.
Take, for example, *a bat*, and fix their attention upon some instance in
which a real bat was flying about the room.   Ask them to recall it and
think how the bat looked.   Do this whenever *new words* for objects
occur in the Lessons, or *whenever they are put in by the teacher* whether
they have been previously given or not.]

LESSON 12.

(Reading.)

Where are the chickens?

Where are the chickens?

There they are. Do look at them!

There they are. Do look at them !

O, see the hen and the chickens !

O, see the hen and the chickens !

How many are there?

How many are there ?

Here is one chicken.

Here is one chicken.

Do you see it?

Do you see it?

(*Writing.*)

Who has the ball?

Who has ___ ___?

George has the ball.

_____ has ___ ___.

Who now has the ball?

Kate has the ball.

Whose ball is it now?

Whose ___ is it now?

It is John's ball.

It is ___ ___.

Dictation.—The fox. See the frog. Here is the cat. Where is the mouse? This is the rat.

[To attract the attention of the children to the thought, and thus divert it from the irksomeness of learning mere language, the teacher may easily make a *real* game of this lesson. Let a *ball*, a *pencil*, a *knife* and a *button* be passed from one to another till no one but the possessor knows who has the objects. Teacher writes upon the board, Who has the ———? (naming any one of the objects). The possessor raises the hand. Children write, Who has the ball? (that being the object named). George raises his hand. Teacher writes, and children imitate, George has the ball. Thus they learn the new idiom, and also how to write their own names.

They should gradually learn such expressions for possession as *John's*, *Kate's*, *my*, *mine*, *your*, *yours*, *our*, *ours*, *his*, *hers*, *its*, *their*, *theirs*. These will be introduced from time to time. The Lessons should increase in interest. Here are two objects, the *possessor* and the *possessed*. For oral practice, and as a preparation for writing, the teacher may ask, What has the *bat!* What has the *fish!* etc., eliciting as answers *wings*, *fins*.

LESSON 13.

(Reading.)

O, see there! a bat!

Do you see the bat?

Yes; I see the bat.

Will the bat bite me?

O no; the bat will catch a fly.

Here is a fly.

Where is the hen?

Here is the hen.

The hen has six chickens.

Can you see the chickens?

Misplaced Objects.

(To be written with the proper objects.)

The bat ------ has ------ horns.

The cow ------ has ------ fins.

The fish ------ has ------ feet.

The dog ------ has ------ wings.

The fox ------ has ------ scales.

[Let the children write, The —— has, and then select a suitable object.]

(Writing.)

Where is my hat?

Your hat is on the table.

Where is ___ ___?

Your ___ is on ___ ___.

What bird is that?

That is a crow.

The crow is on the fence.

O, see that wren!

Where is the wren?

The wren is near her nest.

What has the wren in her bill?

O, see the little wrens!

[The teacher can add interest to the expression for *the place of the object* by putting it successively *over, under, beside, before, behind,* some other object. Thus, Where is the knife? It is *on the table, over the table, under the table.* Resort to every such artifice to make the Lessons interesting to the children. Here again are *two objects,* one *known* and the place of the other fixed by it.]

LESSON 14.

(*Writing.*)

Is this your
top, Ned?
No; it is
George's top.
May I see the top
spin? May I see
_____ _____ _____?

Yes; there! See it spin.
Do you see those
birds fly?

O, see the ducks swim!

O, see ___ ___ ___!

Hark! hear the dog bark!

___! hear ___ ___ ___!

The dog is near the fox.

O, see how they look!

(Place the proper actions with their objects.)

Hear the child ------- bark.

Hear the dog ------- sing.

O, see the mouse ------- fly.

O, see the dove ------- gnaw.

Can you make the top -------

draw?

Can you make the horse

------- spin?

[Let the children have oral practice before writing, and be sure to test their power to *recall*.]

Dictation.—Teacher gives:—Here is my top. Where is your pen? O, see the rat and the cat! etc., etc.

(Reading.)

Who has Jane's ball?
Ann has it. It is in her
hand. Where is my top?
It is under the table.
Who will spin the top?
I will spin it. There!
The cat is near it.
Whose hat is this?
Where is Ned's hat?
His hat is on the table.
Whose hat is that?

That is John's hat.

Can he get it?

No; he cannot get it,

but Tom can.

Who is that? That is Ned.
Whose dog is with him? That is
my dog. Will your dog bite?
Yes, he will bite a rat. There!
see him bite that mouse!

LESSON 15.
(Writing.)

O, see that

tall jar!

Whose jar is it?

It is Mary's jar.

What bird is that? :

It is not a crow, but a jay.

It is ___ ___ ___ ___ __ ___.

Is the jay black?

No; the jay is blue.

How many white doves

have you?

I have three white doves.

The grass is ___.

___ ___ is green.

The sky is ——.

The blue sky is above us.

How many bright stars can you see?

(Writing.)

(Object and quality to be properly united.)

The pig is ------- just.

The crow is ------- white.

The snow is ------- black.

The sky is ------- green.

The grass is ------- blue.

The man is ------- glare.

The ice is ------- foolish.

Dictation.—Let the teacher put together three or four short connected idioms so as to make a little story; thus, The cat is after the mouse. O see the mouse run! There! the cat has him! Will the cat eat him? O yes; she will eat him.

[Lessons may be made more and more interesting as the children learn to *characterize* the objects, or tell how they are in themselves, as *black, white, hard, soft, smooth, rough, long, short,* etc. The idioms for these are learned early. They take two forms, one when the characteristic is prominent, the other when it is incidental.]

LESSON 16.
(Writing.)

Here is a zebra. Did you ever see a zebra?

John, do you hear the
birds sing?

Yes; I hear them sing.

Can you write long words?

No; but I can read
and write short words.

Do you know whose pen
this is?

Give me some bread.

4

Jane wants her little doll.

Let her have her doll.

May we stay at school?

(Reading.)

May I go to school? Yes; you
may go. Can you write? I can
write a little. Can you read what
you write? Yes; I can read what
I write, and what the teacher
writes. Can you write these marks
                              Yes; I write
them every day. I make words
out of them. What do you call
them? I call them word-marks,
but Jane calls them letters.

(Writing and Reading.)

Teacher pronounces distinctly some familiar expression. Children
write it. Then each reads his own. They then exchange slates and
read one another's writing.

[If they are embarrassed, it will help the teacher to see what kind
of drill is needed in penmanship. The children are not yet prepared to criticise one another's work.]

LESSON 17.

(*Writing.*)

The cat can run.

The — can —.

Can — — —?

That girl may read.

That — may —.

May — — —?

This boy must write.

This — must —.

Must — — —?

Charles will go.

Charles ___ ___.

Will ___ ___?

We shall ride.

We shall ___.

Shall ___ ___?

He would come.

He would ___.

Would ___ ___?

You could stand.

You could _____.

Could ___ ___?

[Drill practice will make apparent to the eye the distinctions which the children have long since made intuitively. Add to these exercises in which the *descriptive* words used by children shall come in, such as *good, bad, big, large, little, small, pretty, naughty, nice, funny, jolly.*]

LESSON 18.

(Drill practice in reading and writing.)

Where is ___ ___?

There ___ ___ *is.*

Who is ___ *pretty* ___?

John ___ ___ *nice* ___.

Give ___ *good* ___.

See the little ___ run.

Here are ___ black ___.

Is ___ big ___ here?

O, there ___ old ___!

[Let the children fill the following blanks with any suitable words, and each read from the slate.]

That ___ is tall.

These ___ ___ white.

What ___ ___ ___ do?

Is my ___ ___ in ___ ___?

Can he ___ ___ ___?

O, — — — —!

That tree is near — —.

(Reading.)

Your watch is right. It is on the table. I can see my face in it. Let me take your nice watch. Who has the key? I will wind it. My mamma has a gold chain. May I put her chain on your watch? O, no; she will not let you do it.

———

LESSON 19.

(Reading.)

That tree is tall.

That tree is tall.

O, see those blue birds!

O, see those blue birds!

How many words shall I write?

How many words shall I write?

You may write four words.

You may write four words.

(Writing.)

The robin is a bird.

The ___ is _. ___.

Is this stick a cane?

Is ___ ___ _ ___?

This letter is a, a, *A,* A.

Is this letter small b, b?

Yes; this letter is small b, b.

What letter is this — S?

This letter is large S.

How many letters do you know?

I know ten letters.

[Idioms for telling *what objects are* will come into use every day. " What is it, or what do you call this?" is the question of childhood. Let the teacher present real objects, with the question, " What is this?" All write " It is a ——."]

In this way bring forward the *letters.* They appear in alphabetical order in the next Lesson, to be referred to, but not to be learned as an alphabet at present.

LESSON 20.

THE ALPHABET.

SCRIPT LETTERS.

$\mathscr{A}$	a	$\mathscr{J}$	j	$\mathscr{S}$	s
$\mathscr{B}$	b	$\mathscr{K}$	k	$\mathscr{T}$	t
$\mathscr{C}$	c	$\mathscr{L}$	l	$\mathscr{U}$	u
$\mathscr{D}$	d	$\mathscr{M}$	m	$\mathscr{V}$	v
$\mathscr{E}$	e	$\mathscr{N}$	n	$\mathscr{W}$	w
$\mathscr{F}$	f	$\mathscr{O}$	o	$\mathscr{X}$	x
$\mathscr{G}$	g	$\mathscr{P}$	p	$\mathscr{Y}$	y
$\mathscr{H}$	h	$\mathscr{Q}$	q	$\mathscr{Z}$	z
$\mathscr{I}$	i	$\mathscr{R}$	r		$\&$

LESSON 21.

THE ALPHABET.

ROMAN LETTERS.

A	a	J	j	S	s
B	b	K	k	T	t
C	c	L	l	U	u
D	d	M	m	V	v
E	e	N	n	W	w
F	f	O	o	X	x
G	g	P	p	Y	y
H	h	Q	q	Z	z
I	i	R	r	&	&

[Attention should be drawn to the alphabet gradually. By this time the children have acquired some facility in the use of letters. Thus far they are merely word-marks. Let them gradually become known by name and sound.]

·LESSON 22.

(Review.)

General Exercises.

[These exercises are to be given out by the teacher—not necessarily in this order, not all at one session, especially not *always* the very words here given. Let every review embrace what has been done, but always with *variations* and *additions*, as indicated by the *dash*, or *etc.*]

1. Read Lessons 11, 13, 14, ——, ——, ——.

2. Write [teacher dictates] ox, fox, box, ——, ——, ——, ——; this house, that pen, my hat, ——, ——, ——; Here is the dog. Where is the horse? Who is that? ——, ——, ——, ——, ——.

3. Write any good word for these blanks (teacher writes the blank form on the board). Who has —— ——? Is that a ——? Where —— ——? etc.

4. Pupils give short examples, as, Hear that man scream! etc., etc.; the teacher writes them on the board.

5. Teacher writes *a, m, p, s*, ——, ——, ——, ——, ——, ——, on the board; children write the same on their slates, first small, then capital letters. Children give the names of the letters written.

6. Teacher calls upon any one to give a short word, as pin; she then utters the first sound, writing *p*, then the second, writing *i*, then the third, writing *n*, then she utters *pin*. Class repeat this exercise with other words.

7. Teacher gives the sound of *m* and asks the children to write the letter for it, the same with *a, c, d, p, s* ——, ——, ——, ——, ——. Children name the letters.

8. Teacher writes an example on the board, as,

This is a hen, leaving it for a moment; then removing it she calls upon the class to reproduce it; then they remove and write it again a little quicker, then again, and so on till they write it promptly. Be careful that they write correctly.

LESSON 23.

(Review.)

General Exercises.

Teacher.—All *think* of the object, and *write*—

1. Dove, cat, hen, zebra, pig, boys.
The dog; this horse; that bird; those chickens; these ducks.

2. The little pig; those wild ducks; these young crows; those old wrens.

3. It is a mouse. There is the boy. Here is the man. Who is that?

4. Where is my white hat? O, see the little top spin! Who has John's smooth cane? Whose new pen is this? Where is my nice cap? Here it is.

Spelling.

1. Think of the *object* and of the *word*, and tell me what I shall write for— (Here the teacher pronounces the word, then writes the letters on the board as the children name them.)

2. Teacher names the letters of some familiar word, and the children write the word on their slates.

3. Teacher writes the following examples one at a time, and after erasing asks them to write and *name* the letters in order: In the house; On the top; Here is the cat.

[If any fail, repeat the trial, requiring each to look attentively to the part which was missed.]

—◦◦—

LESSON 24.

Test Exercises.

1. **The copying test.**—In no case, thus far, have the children been called upon to criticise one another's examples. The copying has been done under the *direct inspection* and *guidance* of the teacher. It is best for them at first not to see the imperfect examples which would thus be placed before them. It is to be hoped that they may now, without detriment, examine one another's work by exchanging slates. This test will, however, need the special care of the teacher. It will help the children to *read* varied forms of writing. Let them read the examples thus given them; then let them call attention to any *omissions, defects* or *errors*. This will eventually be as serviceable to the teacher as to the children. Let them review Lesson 14, for example, and exchange slates.

2. **The memory test.**—This presupposes faithful and repeated copying. It may be conducted in various ways, but generally should be mingled with the new lessons. In this the children write from *dictation,* and their success or failure will show their *real* progress.

This will guide the teacher as to the *necessity* of reviews. It is to be conducted by pronouncing distinctly such *words* or *idioms* as are supposed to be familiar or are thus to be made familiar. Let them try any of the first six lessons. Press on this work vigorously.

3. **The mastery test.**—This is an advance upon the preceding. It is conducted by taking the *most familiar* examples and requiring the children to write them with unhesitating readiness. At present few examples may be ripe for it. It is time, however to begin on some of the most frequently written examples. Let the children see who will write them promptly, and yet correctly. It is a stimulating exercise, and hereafter should be resorted to daily.

Exercises.

1. Let the children copy in script letter the reading exercise of Lesson 11, p. 31, thus receiving the thoughts from Roman letters and expressing them in script.

[Here they need not *rules* for capitals, punctuation-marks, etc., but a **well-guided attention** to everything in the prevailing *way* or *fashion* of doing the work. They will seize at once upon what they see as the *way* others do a thing, while the mind shrinks from learning and applying the *rule* for the very same thing. Yet they will soon be able to put into statement their own custom.]

2. In like manner let them copy from pages 38, 45, 50, 55.

[Here let the children exchange slates and compare the written copy with the printed original. Now let them search sharply for any omissions or deviations.]

3. This work being done and cleared from the slates, the teacher *pronounces*, for the memory test, any of the

sentences which they have just written. Thus, without the model before them, they are to express in writing the thoughts they receive through the ear.

[Here teacher and pupils will look carefully to the examples written. A *good habit* is everything in the art of writing.]

4. In a similar way give other sentences containing familiar words.

5. The teacher, knowing what examples are most familiar, will now give out any for *rapid* writing.

6. Teacher now shows them how to put into form a *note* to their teacher, or to any one else, making a simple request; as, for example, to exchange a book, to leave the seat or the room.

[Let them do this from time to time as a real thing.]

Note.—In conducting writing exercises for the purpose of spelling, it is a good plan to call upon the children to write some example; as, "See the fox;" then let them erase it, *think* how they wrote it, and simply *tell* what marks they must make to rewrite it. Thus, large *S*, double *e*, or *e, e* (pronounce or not); space, tee-aitch-e, space, ef-o-ex, period. This shows *what* marks they must make to write it, and that is spelling for *written forms.* This exercise should, at present, be introduced only occasionally. Instead of *naming* the letters, let them give their *sounds*, then *pronounce* and *write* the words. Endeavor to secure variety of exercise in thought, but with it incessant repetition of *form.* Be sure to *reverse* every process—that is, *give* what was *required*, and then *require* what was given.

PART II.

EXPRESSIONS FOR EVENTS.

LESSON 25.

(Writing.)

Bees buzz.

_____ swim.

Birds _____.

Do trees grow ?

Do _____ sleep ?

Do dogs _____ ?

The cat mews.

Cats _____.

Does the boy play ?

Note.—In Part I. the script letter has been given in the text as examples for the children to copy. They have become sufficiently familiar with the forms of the letters to make them at sight. They are hereafter to *remember* the script forms, and make them when other forms are given. It will be well for the children *soon*, if not now, to use *pen* and *ink*.

5

Do the ＿＿＿ spin?

Does the wheel ＿＿＿?

Do the men work?

O, how the wind ＿＿＿!

Do see that horse ＿＿＿!

Let the children write the following words in proper combinations.

Frogs, bugs, hens, cows, robins, fishes, cackle, low, sing, croak, buzz, swim.

[Here we have the *root* of all idioms or sentences for *customary actions*. The children will be interested in learning to *write* what they have already learned to speak so fluently, as, for example, in telling what the *horse*, the *dog*, or the *duck* does. Without naming these distinctions, let them write many examples in the singular and plural, the declarative, interrogative and exclamatory forms.]

(*Review.*)

Children read and write Lessons 6 and 7. Let them write from dictation, O, there is a pig! See that horse. Where is my pen? Who is that? See the zebra run.

Let them read from examples written on the board.

[Add to this list of objects and customary acts. The children must increase their written vocabulary, and should *feel* it an offence against good usage not to begin their sentences with capitals and end them with the proper mark. The teacher has only to *call attention* to real examples to show what the custom is.

Thus, the teacher writes any example, as, Do the men work— and, for a moment, omit the question mark, asking, What mark shall I write here? Let every member of the class decide. In the same way write O, how the dust flies —. See the boys run —. Where are they going —.]

LESSON 26.

(Writing.)

Lions eat meat.

_____ eats worms.

_____ _____ flies.

_____ drink _____.

Larks _____ _____.

The bird feeds her young.

The horse eats _____.

The cows _____ _____.

The _____ drinks _____.

What does the bee make?

What does _____ _____ see?

What do _____ _____ play?

Do dogs gnaw bones?

Do _____ _____ milk?

Does the _____ _____ grass?

O, how the mill grinds the corn!

[Children write and connect properly the following.]

Tigers eat .... water.
Horses drink .... meat.
Hens lay .... their fins.
Birds feed .... ice.
Fishes move .... eggs.
Heat melts .... their young.

[The plan and character of this lesson will need no explanation
to the teacher; but while the children write it faithfully, their attention is not to be called to the *grammatical object* as such, only to the
thought, What does —— eat? Encourage
the children to put in anything else
which the thought admits.]

(Reading.)

There! that cow is here! See how she
eats the corn. Who will run for her?
John! John! drive that cow off. It is
Henry Cook's cow. She is a bad cow.
See the fence. She tears off the rails and
breaks it down. Catch her if you can.

LESSON 27.

(Writing.)

Those boys are running.

Are those ____ ____ ?

What are those ____ doing ?

The wren is feeding the little wrens.

What is the wren ____ ?

The mouse is creeping slily.

The ____ are ____ the cheese.

How is the ____ sleeping ?

The horse ____ ____ swiftly.

(Reading and Writing.)

Teacher writes several examples on the board for the children to read.

Children write from dictation—Birds fly. The hens eat corn. Can the bird sing? O, see the horse run !—and then exchange slates, reading the examples as well as they can, and calling the attention of the teacher to anything that troubles them.

Teacher gives out a few examples for the mastery test (p. 12, 3), a few examples for spelling by writing, tries them on Lesson 19, to see how many letters they can name, and from time to time teaches them to repeat the letters in alphabetical order.

Should any of the combinations be incorrectly made—as, " The hens *is* eating corn"—try to make the children *feel* that the expression does not " *sound* well" when spoken, or " *look* well" when written.

LESSON 28.

(*Reading.*)

The dog barks. Do dogs run? Yes; dogs do run. How many dogs has your brother? He has two dogs and one cat. Do cats bark? O, no! cats mew. What do the birds do? The birds sing, eat, fly and chirp.

(*Reading.*)

REVIEW.

Where is my top? It is under the table. May I spin my top? Yes; you may spin your top on the floor. Who has the ball? Dick has the ball. Let us play ball. Who will pitch the ball? James shall pitch it. Give me the bat. O, it is a bad bat! Let me have John's bat. That is a good one.

[Give review exercises as in previous Lesson.]

LESSON 29.

(*Writing.*)

The birds sang upon the trees.

The ＿＿＿ ran ＿＿＿ ＿＿＿ ＿＿＿.

Did the birds sing upon the trees?

Did the ＿＿＿ fly ＿＿＿ ＿＿＿ air?

O, how the birds sang upon the trees!

O, how the ＿＿＿ rode ＿＿＿ ＿＿＿ sleds!

Where did the boys play ball?

Where were the bees making honey?

O, how the hot sun did burn the grass!

Was the boy writing his lesson well?

Yes; he was writing every word well.

He was reading what he wrote.

[Here two modifications of the idiom will be noticed by the teacher: the *time* is changed and the *place* or *manner* is specified. No *technical* form should be given to the children. They already *apprehend* or *feel* the distinction. It may be *incidentally* noticed as a change in the thought. Take any common objects that act or are represented as acting, such as *ducks, fishes, foxes, bears, sun, moon, water, ice*, and let the children name any action or state. Teacher then assigns a suitable lesson, requiring them to *write* what they *speak*, adding the *place* or *manner* of the event.]

LESSON 30.

(*Writing.*)

James has caught the ball.

Has _____ _____ his lost knife?

Who has caught the ball?

Who has _____ _____ _____?

David had written before we began.

He writes well and reads well.

What had _____ _____ when we came?

Who had _____ _____ _____ _____ at noon?

Have the boys read their lesson?

O, how neatly Jane has done her work!

Charles had not written one word.

(Reading.)

O, see the horse! How he runs! There! he stops by the fence. Who will catch him? I cannot catch him. Here comes Ned. He will catch the horse. O, how the horse tosses his head! Will he kick Ned? O, no; Ned has some oats. Horses like oats. There! Ned has caught the horse. See him eat the oats. Horses should be well fed. Give them hay and grain.

[The teacher will bear in mind any of the past lessons which have not been reviewed sufficiently to *impress* them permanently. Let them be reviewed carefully, but with such changes as will keep the thought fresh. Give *new words* whenever needed.]

LESSON 31.

(Writing.)

The cherries are ripe. You may eat ripe cherries. Unripe fruit will make you sick.

The boys are playing ball. They have formed a club, and have made my brother Joe captain.

Come and take your little sister with you. We shall sail in the boat. Where are you going? We shall sail down the bay.

(Reading.)

Look! there is Kate. What is she feeding? It looks like a little dog No; it is a rabbit.

Do you see his ears? O, what long ears! O, look! look! what a little tail!

Will he bite Kate? O, no; rabbits will not bite any one.

What has Ned done? O, see! see! he has broken his slate.

How did he break it? He fell on the ice as he was coming to school.

See how his nose bleeds. He fell flat on his face, and his nose struck the ice.

Did he cry? Yes; he cried a little, and then came bravely to school.

Ned is a good boy. Let him wash his face. I will give him a slate.

LESSON 32.

(Writing.)

[Let the children fill out the forms from the suggestive questions and blanks, the teacher reading the question if necessary.]

The boys (*are doing what?*).

(*Who?*) are driving the sheep.

The birds are eating (*what?*).

The girls are playing dolls (*where?*).

The (*what kind of?*) birds are singing (*where?*).

The little child sleeps gently (*where?*).

.The. *(what kind of?)* dogs *(do what?)* *(where?)*.

(*Who?*) *(does what?) (how?) (where?)*

_____ _____ can write ____ ____.

____ ____ ____ had come ____ ____.

Has ____ ____ brought ____ ____?

O, how ____ ____ has dried ____ ____!

(*Reading.*)

From the board, from their slates, and from Lesson 29.

(*Dictation.*)

From idioms in Lessons 7, 8, 11.

(*Thought writing.*)

Idioms in Lessons 4 and 6.

[The teacher will find it well to let the class write test examples first slowly and carefully, then a little faster, but with equal accuracy, then let them write still more rapidly, but *never so fast* as to obscure the writing. Their real handwriting is not formed till they write their *thoughts* rapidly and unconsciously.]

·(*Thought reading.*)

Idioms in Lesson 30.

[Teacher writes any familiar example on the board. One or more of the pupils will *read* it. Teacher (removing it) calls upon one or more to *speak* it, and thus compares the two utterances as *a test* of the reading. Repeat this exercise. If speaking is thinking aloud unwritten thoughts, reading is only thinking aloud written thoughts.]

LESSON 33.

When I went to the window, I saw a little bird upon the wall. = When _____ I heard, _____ _____ I _____ (*where?*).

Do you think that he can write this lesson? = Do _____ _____ that _____ _____ _____ (*what?*)?

If it does not rain, George and Alice are going to sail in the boat. = If _____ _____ _____, (*who?*) will come to _____ _____.

Don't blame me till you know what I did. = _____ _____ him till _____ _____ what _____ _____.

Sarah, will you tell me where I may find my doll? = _____, can you _____ _____ when _____ _____ _____ (*where?*)?

Father bought me a ball when he went to Boston. = ____ sold ____ ____ ____ when ____ ____ ____ .

[Let the children read these examples and review Lesson 31. Give dictation exercises and keep up the mastery tests. The teacher will see that (==) denotes a similar idiom, and is not to be written by the pupil. Be careful to note what expressions have become familiar and what have not. Let the former be written with promptness. Let all others be brought forward by frequent reviews or appeals to the memory.]

LESSON 34.

(*Writing.*)

Mother says, "I cannot let you go." = ____ says " ____ ____ ____ ____ ____ ."

"John," said he, "we shall have a jolly time." = " ____ ," said they, " ____ ____ ____ ____ ."

"What are you doing there?" said Peter. = " ____ ____ ____ ____ ____ ?" said ____ .

"Are you going to the great Exhibition?" said Hal.

"No, I cannot go," said Alice.

"I will not part with my nice sled," said Freddy, in a rage. = "_____ _____ _____ _____ _____ _____," said _____ as he came up.

"Where shall we pass the glorious Fourth?" said all the boys as the teacher closed the school. = etc.

"Come with me," added Jack; "I can show you where the fish will bite." = etc.

"Are we waiting here for nothing?" "I hope not," replied Charles, as he walked about slowly. = "You must not" _____ _____ in a low tone.

[Let these examples be written and read. Let no one omit the quotation marks (" "). The teacher will show why they are used.]

LESSON 35.

(*Dictation.*)—Miscellaneous Exercises.

1. Teacher pronounces distinctly, It is a dog; Here is my hat; thus giving some six or more easy sentences such as the pupils can write from memory.

[Encourage the children to write rapidly, but always distinctly. They must try to keep up with their thoughts as in speaking.]

2. Teacher gives the letters for several short words. Pupils write the words.

3. Teacher gives expressions; as, On the floor; In the house; Under the bed; At noon; The pupils write them.

[If they cannot write a particular word, give the letters orally and see if they can write it; if not, write it in full on the board.]

4. Give the sounds of short words, as *fox*, *rat*, *pig*, and let the children write the letters. Reverse this exercise.

5. Let the children tell what letters they would write for any word as the teacher utters it, and thereby cultivate the ear in connection with the letters.

6. Try some of the most familiar expressions given orally for prompt writing.

7. Let the children write any expression which they can recall.

[Encourage the children thus to write any expressions not fully at their command. It is time now for them to feel that they can *venture* a little. It will create a sense of *want* and a determination to *supply* it. They will try; and if they cannot *quite* think of the expression, they will *impress* it more strongly when they get it.]

LESSON 36.

(*Writing.*)—Miscellaneous.

There he goes to the top of the house!

O, see how the kite pulls the string!

"Mew! mew! mew!" said the cat.

Come, come, John, it rains; we must run.

"Do you like figs, Fanny!" said Tom.

These are the plums that came from New York.

Where are the books that I brought to school?

(*Dictation.*)

[Use these as models with many variations.]

Come, Fred, and bring your kite.

Give me your pen and pencil.

6

Where are the boys?

Who will write this lesson best?

O, hear the boys shout!

[Add to these any of the combined idioms, as in Lessons 32 and 33, and use the following as models to be varied for *prompt writing*.]

Is the boy here?	O, see the boat!
See that duck.	Who is there?
Where is Tom?	May I go home?

LESSON 37.

(Writing.)

See George looking for hens' eggs.

See Mary _____ with her doll.

There is Rover carrying a basket in his mouth.

Here is Jane _____ for her mother.

John has come to take the flowers. =

_____ has gone _____ _____ some plums.

Will you send Hal to tell the news? =

Shall _____ come to _____ in your boat.

I found the hat covered with dust. $=$
He ____ left his coat ____ with water.

Starting early in the morning, we reached the lake before noon. $=$ ____ at ____ ____ I ____ ____ ____.

(Dictation.)

Bring me your pen. Call the boys. Where are your slates? White clouds are pretty. Come, Jane, write your lesson.

Here are the ducks that came across the river. See the big duck. How high she holds her head! Where are they going?

(Reading.)
[Take this lesson and the one preceding.]

LESSON 38.

(Reading.)

John has been in the field looking for berries. He has found a dish full. O, how sweet they are! Can I go with him next time?

O, see this bird's nest! I will not touch the eggs. O, what pretty little eggs! There are one, two, three, four white eggs. Hear the birds! How they scream! I will go away.

O, hear the bees! They are swarming. What do you mean by swarming? Just look and you will see. The air is full of bees. The young bees are seeking a new hive. They will soon have a home by themselves. When they leave the old hive, we say they swarm.

(Dictation and Reading.)

Do you see the ducks? Hear them, quack! quack! quack! Give them some corn. O, how fast they swim! There! down goes one of them out of sight!

[Give a spelling exercise in which the children shall *write* words from the *sounds*. Thus, giving the three *sounds* of "dog" ——, ——, ——, they are to give the three letters, **d o g**.

LESSON 39.

(Writing.)

COMBINED IDIOMS.

Ruth has a little lamb, and Ann loves to feed it. = John —— —— —— and Kate —— —— ——.

Ned asked me to go fishing, but I cannot go. = Jane _____ _____ to play dolls, but _____ _____ _____.

We must go in, or we shall get wet. = _____ _____ _____ _____ _____ or _____ _____ _____ _____.

Can you write this lesson? or must I repeat it?

I can read and write a little, but Mary can read and write very well.

"I am going to the circus to-day," said Tom. "But I shall go to school," said Ned.

"When mother comes we shall have a good time." "But she will not come till next week," said Mary. "Very good," said Ann; "can we not wait?"

I want to see her very much. She said she should get me a nice new dress.

(Dictation.)

[Let the teacher urge forward the *memory* and *mastery* exercises.]

LESSON 40.

(*Writing.*)

The dog barks.

The dogs _____.

Where is the horse ?

Where _____ the horses ?

Does the man need help ?

_____ the men _____ _____ ?

This lesson is easy.

_____ lessons _____ easy.

That pen is good.

_____ pens _____ good.

Has the boy returned ?

_____ the boys _____ ?

Henry has written his lesson.

The girls _____ read their _____.

The bird is eating a worm.

The birds _____ eating _____.

This tree is tall.

_____ trees _____ taller _____ these.

What boy broke that tumbler?

What boy has _____ that _____ ?

Does the boy learn?

_____ _____ boys _____ ?

O, how the bees buzz!

O, how the bee _____ !

[Be sure that changes in form are correctly and promptly made.]

LESSON 41.

(Reading and Writing.)

Teacher dictates,—Here is a boy giving a dog some drink.

[Let one of the more advanced pupils go to the board and write; all the rest write at their seats.]

Children read from the board and from their slates.

Teacher calls upon some member of the class to give an example.   All write and read as before.

Teacher writes upon the board three short connected sentences.   Children read.

Teacher gives orally, Here is a little bird. It is a young robin. Who will bring a worm? See how quickly he eats it!

[When a child asks for any one of these words, let the teacher write it on the board. Two problems are always before the child when writing—the *thought* and the *expression*. Give judicious aid in both, that each may respond *promptly* to the other.]

The children give some two or three similar examples; the teacher writes and the children read.

[With children there is always a great advantage in reversing the problem. It gives an insight into both sides of it. They *write* their own thoughts and *read* those of others.

Let each write any sentence that he can recall and read from his slate.

———⚬◦⚬———

LESSON 42.

(*Writing.*)—GENERAL REVIEW.

O, here is a pig in our parlor!

O, ＿＿ an ＿＿ ＿＿ in ＿＿ mill-pond!

Give ＿＿ some bread and ＿＿ for ＿＿ supper.

The books which ＿＿ ＿＿ ＿＿ were very ＿＿.

(Dictation.)

Give me the pen and ink.

_____ him _____ _____ _____ _____.

Where are my _____ _____ _____?

Let me have _____ _____ _____.

Will you send _____ _____ _____ _____?

Who _____ _____ _____ this morning?

[Let the teacher fill these blanks orally.]

(Dictation for Prompt and Ready Writing.)

Come, boys, let us have a good play.

Where shall we go?

We will go to the nice lawn.

So we will, but I must get my hat.

May my brother Joe go with us?

Yes; and Sam too.

What shall we play?

We shall play ball, of course.

Have you a good bat?

Yes; I have a good one.

(*Writing.*)

To Arrange Words Properly.

The bear the garden is in.

Is where my brother's horse?

The hill on is a tree tall.

Give your sister to a small ring.

LESSON 43.

(*Reading.*)

See the bright moon in the west.

Hear the birds sing in the grove.

Where shall we eat our nice lunch?

Who will bring us some spring water?

What can we find in the meadow?

That man brought his son with him.

Will you let me read next?

Why ought you to learn to read?

I can write my name in my book.

My mother says I can read very well.

I have been at school only four months.

Do you not like to write our nice lessons?

The teacher gives us new lessons every day.

She told my mother that I should soon write a letter.

I wish I could write a letter to-day.

Where is the thimble? I want to sew my torn frock.

Have you any thread? O, yes, but it is black, and my frock is white.

The rabbit is eating clover.

Who will bring me some fresh milk?

O, hear the drums beat!

What are the boys doing with those poor little birds?

When the rain is over, father and I are going into the woods for nuts.

"George," said Mary, smiling, "will you bring your basket full of nuts?"

"Yes," said George, "and you shall have half of them."

PART III.

EXPRESSIONS FOR CONNECTED EVENTS.

(Stories.)

LESSON 44.

[Let the children first read from the book, then copy carefully, making all the points and breaks for the paragraphs.]

THE RABBIT.

[Story as *written*, to be read and written by the pupils.]

Bunny was a little rabbit. He had long ears and a short tail. His home was in the thick

bushes, and his house was in the ground. Early
one morning his mother went out to gnaw the
bark from the shrubs, but she told Bunny to
stay in his house.

As soon as the mother was away Bunny said
to himself, "I have been shut up in this dark
hole all my life. Why should I not have a good
time and run among the bushes?" So out he
came, happy as a lark, and skipped among the
thick shrubs.

Soon he heard a strange sound. "What is
that?" said Bunny as he pricked up his long
ears. It was the dog chasing the rabbit back to
her safe home. Poor Bunny! As he ran back
for his home he lost his way among the bushes,
and at last fell into the jaws of his and his
mother's worst foe.

The little ones who disobey their mothers are
sure to meet with trouble.

Teacher writes any short story on the board. Children copy the
same, then read as above. Let the children copy any of the previous lessons in like manner, putting in every mark required.

[Let the children exchange slates after writing this, and read
from one another's slates. They should notice and mention any
deviations from the printed example. The more they copy, the surer
they are to observe distinctions.]

LESSON 45.

THE SELFISH PIG.

[Story as *narrated*,—to be heard, written and read by the pupils.]

Now I will tell you a little story. I wish you all not only to *hear* it, but to *tell* it on your slates, and then *read* it to me.

[Here the teacher relates in short sentences the story, of which these are the points: Years ago—in Maine—Uncle George kept three little pigs—the largest, called Grouty—was cross—would bite and drive off the other two when fed —would eat up everything—and let the two go hungry—grew fat—they became lean. One day Uncle George had some friends come on a visit —so he killed Grouty because he was fat. Thus the selfish pig got his reward.]

Teacher tells some fresh story having a local interest; thus the children learn to report in writing what they hear.

Note.—It is of the first importance that children learn to grasp a story in its *fullness*, and to *narrate* it in *their own language*. At first it will be best that one or more narrate it separately, so as to call attention to omissions and defects. In writing let the point be to *make it interesting, to tell it all with life.* The children should read each one his own, and all judge who has told the story well. The teacher will notice that there should be at least three breaks or paragraphs in this story. Let the children get in the way of putting all *little stories* under the one main story by themselves as *parts* of the whole.

LESSON 46.

THE ANTS.

[Story as told partly by Clara and partly by Eva; to be *read* as it is, then to be written in substance by the children and read as their own narrative.]

Clara. Come with me, Eva, and see those little bugs creeping around on that pile of sand.

Eva. Do you call these little things *bugs*, Clara?

Clara. Yes, Eva; I thought they were bugs.

Eva. O, no, Clara; they are *ants.*

Clara. Ants! My ants Mary and Lucy are as big as my mother. They are not bugs! They talk and eat. They never creep around in the sand, but walk as I do, only they are larger than I am.

Eva. O, you mean *aunts!* When we talk, we speak them both alike; but when we write what you call *bugs*, we write *ants*, and the other *aunts.* Now let me see you write the word for your —— Mary.

Clara. O, now I see where I was wrong. There are two kinds of ——, one *ants*, the other *aunts*. But these ants are so busy! O, see that one tugging at that little bit of sand! O, how he pulls!

Eva. Yes, Clara, they are never idle. These little busy ants have built up what you call that pile of sand; it is really an *ant-hill*. There are more little grains of sand than you can count.

Clara. O, Eva, do you mean to say that these little ants have made all this big hill?

Eva. Yes, Clara; and they teach us, if we will be busy every day in doing something good, in the end we may show something more wonderful than this.

Let the children tell this story in three parts (paragraphs).

1. What Clara thought the ants were, and what she called her own aunts.

2. How Eva corrected Clara by showing her how to *write* the two words.

3. What they both observed, and said.

7

[First, let one, two or more tell orally each part. The teacher will guide them.

Next, let them tell the story by making themselves act the part of the *writer*, thus, " Come with me, Eva," said Clara, " and see those little bugs," etc.]

Note.—It is assumed at this stage that the children have acquired some *freedom* in writing out their thoughts. If so, they have called upon the teacher for *many expressions* not contained in the Lessons. This is as it should be. The special demands for language depend so much upon locality, occupation, and special surroundings that no *book* can furnish a vocabulary suited to every case. In writing as in speaking children must be *told* what language to use and how to use it. How do you *write* so and so? is exactly parallel to " How do you *speak* or *say* so and so?" and this is the ever-recurring question of children. They need practice in all the various ways in which thought is represented to the eye. In this last lesson *two* are represented as talking to each other. Let the children learn to gather up these thoughts and tell the story as their own. In every such change they should show by the tones of voice in reading that they recognize the several parties concerned.

LESSON 47.

RHYMING GAME.

[Partly by Kate and partly by Jane just as they told it; to be read and imitated by the children in a similar game with *cat, jar, plate.*]

Kate. I have something that rhymes with bed.

Jane. Is it my little brother ?

Kate. No ; it is not Ned.

Jane. Is it what some one has just spoken?

Kate. No; it is not said.

Jane. Is it what the old bird has done for her young?

Kate. No; it is not fed.

Jane. Is it the color of that rose?

Kate. No; it is not red.

Jane. Is it what we say when a bird has gone?

Kate. No; it is not fled.

Jane. Is it what we do to help a little child?

Kate. No; it is not led.

Jane. Is it what Flora says of her poor father?

Kate. No; it is not dead.

Jane. Is it what we put upon a bed?

Kate. No; it is not a spread.

Jane. Is it what we eat.

Kate. No; it is not bread.

Jane. Is it what Tom and I use in sliding down the hill.

Kate. Yes; it is a sled.

LESSON 48.

FANNY AND HER DOLL.

[Story told by the writer, but in Fanny's own words; to be read by the children and then *written*, each child distinguishing Fanny's words from the writer's.]

"Mother," said Fanny, "you know the little doll, Peep, which you gave me on my birthday?" The tears standing in her little blue eyes, she added: "I went down to the brook to show dollie how the water dashed on the stones."

"As I bent down," she sobbed out, "to pick up a white pebble, my doll slipped from my hand and fell into the brook."

"I cried out," she said, "'O, Peep! Peep! come to me!' but the swift stream carried her down into the thick swamp. She went out of sight and is lost."

"Oh, mother! mother!" she cried ; "what shall I do? She was the nicest doll I ever saw. I never can have another so good! I ought not to have taken her down to the brook. When I thought of what you told me, that I must not go near the swift stream without my brother, I cried and felt sorry that I had been naughty."

"And now, my dear mamma," she said, "I will be a good girl, and not disobey you. Please forgive me this time, and I shall remember what you tell me."

Note.—The teacher should be careful at this stage not to give the children anything like a solitary and discouraging task of find-ing out (inventing) what to say about a subject. Their thoughts should flow so freely as to create a demand for expression.

To this end writing should follow an animated conversation be-tween teacher and pupils. The ideas developed should then be written while fresh in mind, and that without any formal arrangement. Give the children *experience* in thinking, arranging, and writing, and then attention may gradually be drawn to the matter of method.

Let the children now be encouraged to tell some story about what they really saw, and let this be written by all. Perhaps some will like to give it as a dialogue.

It is important for them to become familiar with *all* the methods of representing thought, whether by continued narrative, by dia-logue, by quotation of the actual language of others, or by the incorporation of it without quotation.

LESSON 49.

THE HAWK AND THE STRAY CHICKEN.

[Story written by the children as heard from the teacher; to be read by each, and to be noted with reference to *fullness* of detail.]

Teacher tells the children a story to be written on their slates. The following are the points:

[A farmer had been annoyed by a hawk. One day a hen with her chickens was at a little distance from the barn. Suddenly she called the chickens; all but one gathered around her. This one stood upon the fence some distance off. Soon the hawk appeared just above the barn. The hen called louder and louder, but the careless little chick did not heed her. In a moment down came the hawk and took the chicken in his claws. Just at this time the farmer, who had seen the hawk in the dis-

tance and seized his gun, hiding behind some bushes, rose up and shot the hawk just as he began to fly off with his prey. Thus the chicken, with some cruel scratches, came back to its mother.]

———◦◦◦———

LESSON 50.

WHAT WE SAW AND FELT.

[Pupils come in from recess full of excitement. They had been permitted to go a little distance to a cool spring; near the spring was a clump of hazel-bushes; here the hornets had built a nest. One of the boys threw a stone at the bushes, not knowing that the hornets were there. A great buzzing followed. Soon Kate Jones cries out, "O, how he *bites!*" then Tom Gray, "O, I am stung!" and off they all rush for the school-room. The teacher calls them to order and allows them to tell the story.]

She tells them about the habits of the hornet, and tells them to write their story. Instead of this, as it cannot be *real* to the present class, let any one tell any story of what he really *saw.*

Note.—The most important point—that which should be placed above all others—is to give *freshness* and real *zest* to the written narration. Keep up the two corresponding processes of reading and writing, prompted always by the impulse of thought. Children have an *intense interest* in what they *see* and *tell* for themselves.

Let the teacher *read* some interesting story, and then let the children report in writing all that they can remember of it.

———

LESSON 51.

THE SAIL.

[Let the children *read* this as a distinct lesson, and then *copy* it for a second reading. Be careful that they put in the quotation marks and understand their full significance.]

"Come," said Tom, "you will never be ready. Our sailboat has been waiting a whole hour."

"I have been urging Biddy to get our lunch put up," said Joe. "You know we are to stay at Sandy Beach till two o'clock, and we shall be hungry before we get home."

"I beg your pardon," said Tom; "I never thought of lunch, and we shall be four miles from the town."

"Besides," said Joe, "our skipper has gone to get the rudder mended. We must wait a full half hour for him. But we shall have enough to do to get everything ready on board the boat."

"Good-bye," said the boys as they started for the wharf; "if the tide is not against us, you may expect us home at five;" and off they started for a sail down the bay.

A brisk wind from the north brought them to Sandy Beach in less than two hours. "There!" said Joe; "when did this famous craft ever sail faster?" "We are here early enough," replied Tom; "and now for our bath."

It was one of those hot days in July when a bath in salt water is most refreshing. "How cool the water is!" said Joe as he dashed in, plunging headlong under the surface.

"That is well enough for you," said Tom— "you can swim; but I prefer to stay here, where the water is not deep."

"O, you will never learn to swim," said Joe, "unless you venture more than all that. Come to me, and I will show you how to swim."

"O, do!" said Tom; "that is just what I want."

"O, O, O!" he cried as Joe dashed him under the water; "you will—"

Let the children put this story into a dialogue between Tom and Joe, putting in the writer's thoughts as if spoken by one of them, and completing the story as each may fancy it ended.

LESSON 52.

BAT STORY.

[Story told by the writer as it occurred, to be read by the children, and then written from memory with all books closed.]

Little Amy was a good, bright child, who was busy all day, both working and playing. And when night came, she would go to bed so tired that soon after her little head touched the pillow she would fall asleep.

But one very hot night in July she could not go right off to sleep, though her window was wide open to let in the air. As she lay there trying to keep her eyes shut she heard a strange noise in the room. Amy was not a timid girl, but this noise made her heart beat fast.

Something kept hitting the walls of her room and then the ceiling, and she thought she heard a pair of wings flap, as if a large bird was in the room. She tried not to think about it, when very soon she felt something brush across her face, and she screamed aloud.

Just then the moon came out from behind a cloud and shone in at her window. She saw by the light it gave that a large black object was flitting about the room, first to one side and then to the other. Amy cried, "O, father! father! here is a great, big bird in my room! Do come and catch it."

Her father came in with a light, and shutting the door and window began to chase Amy's bird around the room. But as soon as he had a good, fair look at it he said, "Why, my little girl, that is no bird; it is a bat, Amy."

When the bat was caught, he brought it to her and showed her what big wings it had, and said, "No wonder you could not sleep. A bat makes a great noise in a room."

Amy thought it was very ugly, and said she would never have a bat for a pet so long as she lived.

So the bat was put out of the window, and before long Amy fell into a good sound sleep.

Let the children *narrate* some story which they have *heard.* Let it be the subject of a conversation, and thus let it be prepared to be written for the next exercise.

LESSON 53.

BEAR STORY.

[Story told by the writer in substance as Uncle Ralph told it orally to him; to be read, and then narrated by the children with the books closed.]

Uncle Ralph was a famous woodsman. He lived in Vermont when the country was new. Besides a little land which he tilled, he owned a large forest, in the midst of which he had built a sawmill.

He said that he was at work at his mill one day in the spring and had just begun to saw a huge pine log. It was about noon. He had taken out his tin pail, in which was his dinner. For a moment he placed it upon the log through which the saw was slowly cutting its way. He then stepped into the shed near by, not knowing what pair of eyes was watching his steps.

As he came out to see how much work the saw had done, to his great surprise a large bear was mounted on the log with his back to the saw, quietly eating up the hungry man's dinner. It was of no use to oppose. The dinner was fast going. It may be, he thought, the bear will have the worst of it, after all. Bears are not used to sawmills.

As the saw moved up and down it began to tickle the bear's tail. "Ugh!" growled old Bruin. Soon it began to scratch him severely. Then, turning around and rising up, he fiercely seized the saw with his teeth. Poor bear! he lost his dinner. In a moment, as the saw came down, it took away all relish for his stolen repast, and sent him tumbling from the log.

Teacher reads some story like that of Putnam and the wolf, conversing about it and answering questions, then gives it to be written and read. It is to be the reading lesson for the next day.

LESSON 54.

A LETTER.

[Story told by Susie in Providence to her mother in Boston.]

PROVIDENCE, *May 1, 1877.*

Dear Mamma:

You cannot think how much I have missed you since you went away. It seems as if you had been gone a year instead of a week.

I have done everything you told me to do, and papa says I have been a good little girl. I have dusted the parlor every morning, and filled the vases with flowers, just as you always do when here.

One morning, after feeding my canary-bird and giving it fresh water, I raised one of the windows in the room to let in the cool air. Then I went away, and did not come back again for some time. When I did come in, what do you think I saw? The cage door wide open and my birdie gone. I did not fasten the door securely, I suppose, and that is how it happened. I feel so sorry.

Come home, do, dear mamma, before I get too lonesome.

Your loving daughter,

Susie.

Let the children turn the Bear Story, Lesson 53, also the substance of Lessons 46, 48, 50 and 51, into letters.

Let them write letters about some interesting occurrence at school to some absent friend. The teacher will guide them in respect to details.

Suggestions.—At this stage, the children who have followed the course faithfully have acquired considerable facility in writing their thoughts. If in the exercises their own simple thoughts have found free expression, somewhat as when they speak, they have already begun to enjoy the work.

A genuine *relish* for writing and reading is the *vital point* to be gained. This will increase as the children see in their work something *real* and *practical*. The all-absorbing impression that they are expressing their thoughts takes away the feeling of fatigue and disgust arising from the constant repetition of muscular action or of mental effort in making and recognizing the same forms.

The nearer this *repression* approaches to that of the corresponding efforts in speaking and hearing, the better will be the work; and the nearer the *frequency* of writing and reading approaches to that of oral intercourse, the more certain the success. To this end a Second Book in Thought and Expression is arranged to keep up continued practice in *all forms of writing* in connection with the school exercises and the affairs of life.

It will be easy for the teacher to call attention to any needed points in what they write, regarding the words *as language* (not expression of thought). Thus, the alphabet, the sounds of the letters, the syllables of the words, the order of the letters in the words, the penmanship, the difference between capital and small letters, the punctuation-marks, the order of words in idioms, their change of form, etc., etc., all of which they are to notice as what they have made without thinking at the time *why* they did it. They will thus *evolve* from their own good habits the practical rules for their guidance.

.

www.ingramcontent.com/pod-product-compliance
Lightning Source LLC
Chambersburg PA
CBHW031441280326
41927CB00038B/1488